to "Cowboy"
Langford —
In grateful thanks
for the loan of
your portrait

Phebe

(page 83)

21st Century Dog

21st Century Dog

A Visionary Compendium

Edited by Michael J. Rosen

with commentary by Michael J. Rosen and Mark Allen Svede

Stewart, Tabori & Chang
New York

Compilation and introduction copyright ©
2000 Michael J. Rosen

Designed by David Butler, Art of the Midwest

Art at right by Anne Watkins
Art at far right by Stephen Webster

Published in 2000 by
Stewart, Tabori & Chang
A division of U.S. Media Holdings, Inc.
115 West 18th Street
New York, NY 10011

Distributed in Canada by General Publishing
Company Ltd.
30 Lesmill Road
Don Mills, Ontario, Canada M3B 2T6

Library of Congress Cataloging-in-Publication Data
21st century dog : a visonary compendium / edited by
Michael J. Rosen.
    p. cm.
    "Future dog!—an exhibition of contemporary draw-
ings ... reserved for display in St. Louis, Missouri,
beginning on October 1, 2000"—CIP galley p. 123
    ISBN 1-58479-041-5
    1. Dogs—Caricatures and cartoons—Exhibitions. 2.
American wit and humor, Pictorial—Exhibitions. 3.
Dogs—Forecasting—Exhibitions. I. Title: Twenty-first
century dog. II Title: At head of title: Future dog. III.
Rosen, Michael J., 1954–
NC126.A142000
741.5'973—dc21   00-030113

Printed in Italy

10 9 8 7 6 5 4 3 2 1

First Printing

This book is dedicated to a better future for dogs and, while we're at it, people, too, especially the nine who welcomed the new millennium around the bonfire at Hopewell Springs.

CONTENTS

Now, Next, *and* Never Mind

O n the auspicious eve of the turning century, ten friends gathered around a bonfire in the snow-blanketed meadow overlooking our pond. While we each inscribed pieces of paper to ceremoniously cast into the fire before midnight on December 31, 1999—all those thwarted quests, nagging irritations, perennial worries or woes, and lingering fears that we longed to leave behind with the passing year—the three dogs in attendance (Madison, Ticker, and their cousin Maggie, who was sleeping over) danced around our half circle, dove through drifts, cavorted along the frozen banks—doing whatever simply being together right then and right there suggested. Which was, not surprisingly, what they did the previous time they were together. Which is, most likely, what they'll do the next time they get together.

Just after midnight, the ten of us jotted down our aspirations for the new year, our dreams of prosperity and fulfillment and so forth, and tossed those slips into the tepee of flames whose sparks floated upward in the cold air, as though to convey our hopes heavenward, adding their influence to the presiding constellations. The three dogs did not feign interest in these wish-filled prescriptions. Yet, by then, the dogs were happy enough to sit for photographs, panting with their bright red gums and snowy goatees, circulating among the huddled couples as if to remind us all that nothing much has changed since the first *Homo sapiens* and the first canids shared a fire.

If the dogs *had* participated in the bonfire, dictating the hopes of Dog in general for the coming era, what might they have wanted us to inscribe on our slips? Guesses include:

Lower handles on refrigerators

No breed restrictions at fox hunts

More cheese, and, since we're thinking kitchen, figure out how to make
*   good-for-dogs chocolate*

Microwave popcorn on demand

Liver bits that aren't already soggy or linty from the show handler's mouth
*   and pockets and a little less groping from the ring judges*

Move the Iditarod someplace balmy

Our own companion animals—preferably wearing a uniform

A telepathic human who can understand and arrange for all these
*   demands before the next millennial bonfire*

Dogs understand Now. Happy dogs, treated to the bliss of routine, surely understand Next—as in, *After they have Lunch, we have Plates to lick;* or *After they have Post Office, we have a Ride, and then Thank-You-for-Waiting Jerky Treats.* But they show no recognition of the future tense, even though I try to suggest things that are just ahead, particularly when I ask them to endure a dull morning of writing or a longer wait in the car. "We are going to Grandma's house *in a little while.*" "Your friend Mark is coming home *tonight!*" But, instead of waiting, of realizing something is coming later, the dogs instantly spring to attention Now!—though Grandma and Mark are nowhere in sight. It's a version of the old adage: point out something to a dog and he sees your finger.

So are dogs ready for the future? If my own two are any example, the answer is, unequivocally, *Who cares?* As with color, dogs may have some sense of the future, but they have no interest in it. It's only the moving black-and-white reality of the present—the "right here" with the pack—that engages them. Their Year-at-a-Glance planners read: Now, Next, Never Mind. Come tomorrow, come another year, decade, century, or millennium, dogs offer the same stalwart and endearing qualities, while we—reluctantly, childishly, recklessly, or maniacally—race ahead, abandoning so much of the generosity, comfort, attentiveness, and empathy we humans have egocentrically prided ourselves upon. Who's been the bad boy or bad girl?

If we had read aloud those slips of paper tossed into the bonfire before and after the clock struck midnight—those appeals for less time away, less overcommitment, less rushing around, more time just being together, more chances to simply enjoy the stuff of life that yet-more-money can't provide—we would have been able to see that all of us, even the cat people in our group, want more of a dog's life. We want to savor Now, to bask in the delights of Next, and to purchase a big rubber stamp with which to slap "Never Mind," like a muddy dog print, across the piles of obligations and demands already gathering forces while we toast our friendships and fortunes.

For those of us who can't yet have a dog's good life, we have dogs to give us hope for that future possibility.

Whether it tags along like an adorable puppy who—you *swear*—followed you home by accident, or whether it menaces you like the neglected yard dog who charges at you every time you venture down the street, the future is something each of us must recognize and reckon with, and so, in turn, must our dogs, since we are their Fates, determining most every knot or loop in their short leash of life. *Caveat canis*: let the dog beware.

For centuries, changes in dogdom were probably few. Less work, perhaps. Fancier digs. Better kibble. More peculiar-looking cousins. (Just since 1954, the year my first dog, Freckles, and I shared the crib, the AKC has recognized thirty-eight new breeds.)

But recent decades have been saturated with patents, new products, and refinements in nearly every area of canine life. Dogs now enjoy anti-inflammatory drugs, automatic watering devices, variously flavored tennis balls, implanted ID chips, and Frosty Paws "ice cream." In this forty-five-year period, dogs have seen hotels forbid their presence, and then, in an about-face, entice their owners with Very Important Pet programs featuring Waterford crystal water bowls and baked dog bones iced with the "guest's" name.

Never one to spare my dogs a single advantage or advancement, I've sampled the future's newfangled offerings: Pawrier, a bottled water for dogs; puppy kindergartens and day camps; CPR for dogs classes; Dr. Bach's Rescue Remedy to help relieve thunderstorm anxiety (which works). Recently, I read part of Dr. Janet Ruckert's book, *The Four-Footed Therapist,* which recommends using one's own pet as a therapist "to avert illness amid times of change or stress, to strengthen self-esteem and well-being." Now, I had swell dogs as a child, but not once did my parents ever suggest I try such a session during my preteen years, when I (and most every adolescent I knew) would have gladly subjected the family dog to an embarrassing therapy session for even an hour's worth of self-esteem. For one thing, no dog was ever allowed on Mother's couch.

Some of the doctor's exhortations are already integral operations in our present household: daily exercise; familiar routines; talking to the dogs. (She mentions nothing of singing your dog's praises in operatic voices, adapting commercial jingles to rhyme with the dog's nicknames, and delivering a stand-up monologue that extols all the dog's superlative qualities—but I happen to know these also help.)

Yet a few of Dr. Ruckert's suggestions failed us—or we failed them. For instance, to "replenish diminished feelings of self-worth . . . remind you that you are lovable, and serve as a link to your positive childhood experiences," the doctor suggests, "look into your pet's eyes and tell it how important it is to you. Praise its looks, its character, its intelligence."

I got as far as hunkering down and staring into Madison's eyes—an innate signal of aggression and dominance among dogs—before he looked away sheepishly and walked out of the room. Did this mean he sensed that his patient was beyond help?

When I tried this technique with Ticker, he commenced licking my face. I attempted to sustain my litany of praises, so Ticker threw himself utterly into the washing, which indeed reminded me of a childhood experience, albeit a less than positive one: my mother dunking her napkin into her water glass to scrub my face before I could leave the table.

We had further trouble with another of Dr. Ruckert's exercises: collaborating with your dog in the creation of a personal collage. The idea is to "sit with your pet, and cut out dozens of pictures from magazines that reflect your personality and interests. Then paste them onto a large sheet of cardboard . . . and reflect upon what you see." Of all the dogs I've had, my two much-missed golden retrievers showed the most interest in magazines. Carey favored them right after I'd leave the apartment for classes. He would shred my various subscriptions (and books, record albums, college notebooks, what have you) and I would attempt to reassemble them upon return. In retrospect, I suppose this was, indeed, a collaborative form of self-expression: Carey shared his separation anxiety and I shared my collegiate temper.

Paris, my second golden, liked magazines (and original artwork, photographs, and letters) only as the mail carrier shoved them through the slot in the door, under which he napped each morning. But once the magazines were teeth-marked as "received," Paris never again demonstrated the slightest interest in a glue stick or in the creative rearrangement of these scraps.

As for Ticker and Madison's collage experience, they lay beside me for a moment or so. Ticker sniffed a few cologne inserts, then hopped back on the bed. Madison hovered a bit, then lay across the poster board as if to say, in perfect art historical French, *Voila! C'est fini.*

Can I help but wonder if this next century will really improve life for dogs? Or will we find ourselves asking our companions for the umpteenth time in our short and fumbling existence to once again improve our own lives? So wonder I did, with the particular encouragement and commission of the American Kennel Club Museum of the Dog, which asked that I curate an exhibit that would cap a year's survey of the dog in art, from the past to the present and onward toward this just dawning twenty-first century.

Of course, I had nothing equivalent to the scientific models that, say, meteorologists or eco-geo-astro-physic-ologists employ when they predict whatever impending scenario they're asked to plot. No, as in previous books I've edited, I looked to some of the artists and writers I most admired and knew to be—or suspected of being—dog people, and posed a series of questions: What new jobs will dogs be bred to do? What new breeds could you imagine, considering how humans have continually shaped the dog to suit our purposes, notions of beauty, and living spaces? Will dogs be more involved in society, and, if so, what responsibilities will they have? What might improve their lot, their looks, their usefulness?

Their answers comprise this book, and the questions they, in turn, raise are left to each of us to consider. But, at least for now, just enjoy the present volume, the dog at your side, the smell of "yes, it's microwave popcorn!" popping in the next room, and simply never mind.

In the future Dogmocracy,
some pundits argue that dogs
will retain their instincts and
innate skills, resolutely preserving
their canine nature;
others foresee a subtle or even a
not-so-subtle shift in the role
dogs play in our lives, recognizing
that many dogs' greatest instincts
and innate skills have conspired
all along to imitate human nature.

After eons of watchful, focused desire, dogs will—slowly, and not all that gracefully—sprout thumbs. On all four paws, right where the dewclaws have been waiting. Jubilation Day.

This development will call for some thoughtful negotiation. Dogs have waited a long time to achieve grasp, and they will want to use it—on food stored in Tupperware, on car doors, on the TV clicker. Keys. Any nearby wallet. They will argue for equal access, for if they acquire thumbs, language won't be far behind. It will be up to the humans of the future to point out that new privilege entails new responsibility. No card games until the coffee table is dusted—and well, too, into those low-down crevices. No sitting in the car until the breakfast dishes are put away. No TV—don't ask me twice—until teeth have been brushed. Somebody has to do these things while the humans, their new tails held high, go out and pee in the backyard.

Erin McGraw

Benoît

Danny Shanahan

GRRRRR

Shanahan

Throughout the years, Jack's greatest pleasure was to hear the morning newspapers. His loved ones had never considered Jack's blindness an inconvenience and were always happy to oblige him. Despite their willingness, they couldn't always be there for Jack, and some of their voices did grow softer and harder to hear. Often, Jack went without the morning news. Of course, there were Braille versions available as well as smarty-pants broadcasters to dish out the day's events. But Jack grew nostalgic for the good old days of joyful dialogue over the latest stories.

At the turn of 2071, Jack received one of the first of a new breed of sight-assistance dogs: a canine companion that could answer the phone with delightful and witty greetings, remove embarrassing coffee stains off T-shirts, and, yes, even read the morning paper with insightful and thought-provoking commentary.

Hank turned out to be a revolutionary new pup. Jack and Hank would lounge in the park from sunup until teatime, reading and discussing the news from each of the town's daily rags. Although they sometimes squabbled over politics (Jack being a strict conservative, and Hank considering himself a devout follower of the more controversial Green Party), Jack was never seen without Hank, or with a coffee stain on his shirt.

Matthew Yokom

A Brief History of the Talking Dog

In the first decade of the century, the advent of talking appliances, talking cars, and talking spoons and forks whetted consumers' appetites for the ultimate high-tech innovation: talking dogs. In the race to breed a canine that could not only fetch but kvetch, Stanford DNA scientist Dr. Harlan Watson used as his template the most successful talking dog on record: Astro Jetson.

Years of laboratory work proved fruitless, until one day the tenacious scientist was awakened by the following message over his laboratory intercom: *Ratson! Rome rere! Ri reed rou!*

Once the irritating speech impediment was bred out, owners were delighted with the convenience these chatty beasts afforded them. It was a pleasure, for example, to ask a Labrador not only to retrieve a newspaper, but also to read it aloud.

Soon, however, it became apparent that talking dogs had one major disadvantage: owners could not attribute emotions to them as they did to their yowling predecessors. A risk arbitrageur who was used to pouring his heart out to his sympathetic basset hound, for example, was somewhat deflated when his genetically engineered Jack Russell terrier responded, *Like I care?* By mid-century, other drawbacks became painfully apparent. Dog rappers dominated the charts, chanting disparaging rhymes about their bitches. Gambling dogs with Runyonesque hats and ties were no longer cute: they were foul-mouthed louts who called each other *jackass* and *douche bag*.

Scientists spent the latter half of the century looking for ways to get dogs to shut up.

Andy Borowitz

Violet...cook! Good dog.

Violet...clean! Good dog.

Violet...carpool! Very good dog.

Janet Stevens

The passing of the millennium did not bring the anticipated tragedies of the Y2K bug or an onslaught of radioactive mutant aliens, but another more insidious plague: *socks*—left socks, to be precise—began to vanish from dryers on a global scale. A breed of notorious trolls, who previously had worked on a cottage-industry scale, organized via the Internet and prepared to ransack Earth of its left socks, in an attempt to bring the paired-sock world to its knees.

Fortunately, mini-hounds, who had been long out of work due to the decline in mole hunting, were once again in heavy demand, sniffing out the missing footwear. They were uniquely able to descend a dryer's exhaust pipes, shimmy along the maze of tunnels, and burst into the trolls' besocked and besotted lair.

The dryer trolls, once caught, became outcasts in the troll community, forced to take up marginal hobbies, such as darning. The dogs, as always, returned to a hero's welcome.

Paul Lindhorst

Mary Lynn Blasutta

Many prognosticators
suggest that dynamic changes
are likely as dogs fulfill
their evolutionary potential.

Some have even wondered
what place humans might
hold in the new Dogdom,
hoping that this place
isn't a ratty old bath mat
bunched up next
to the refrigerator and given
the absurd name "your bed."

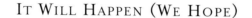

It Will Happen (We Hope)

Somewhere in France, a few years ago, as a boy was pulling up weeds in a family vineyard, he noticed a small leather-bound book in the upturned soil. He ran and brought the book to his father, who, even with his new glasses, could not read the unfamiliar writing. The book languished in a kitchen drawer until a relative, visiting, looking for a salad fork, came across the book and, with casual curiosity, opened it. Since this relative worked in Paris, in a museum that contained many unusual objects, he was able to read it. A fragment of the first paragraph has been translated into English and I offer it to you, as follows:

Arthur Yorinks

In the Twenty-First Century, I Predict
by Nose Stradamus

Having lived among people for these many years, I, Nose Stradamus, commonly known as Fly, a Border collie by birth, now commit to paper my thoughts of what is to be. In the first year of the new millennium, after convening by phone (skill in the use of telephones will have already been accomplished through the correspondence course given by the one known as Old Hemp), it will be decided that the poodle breed will take over the world. Poodles will gain this power by cleverly inserting themselves into local governments and making a series of zoning decisions all across the continents. These decisions, altering land use, which in turn will alter the priorities of the human experience, will only allow for meadows, clean sidewalks, curbs when possible, flowers, houses with plenty of cushions large enough for the largest dog, unfettered access to backyards, and bakeries. Baked goods will be free and available to all . . .

As you read this, experts are struggling to translate the remainder of the first paragraph and what is believed to be the even more important second paragraph, for indeed the millennium is upon us. And have you looked a poodle in the eye lately?

"YOUR WORK'S FINE, IT'S YOUR BREAK TIME I WANT TO TALK TO YOU ABOUT."

Charles Barsotti

"COME ALONG, EDGAR, IT'S TIME TO
GO BACK TO THE OFFICE."

"I CURSE THE DAY I EVER
HEARD OF GINKGO BILOBA."

"WHEN THE GUESTS ARRIVE YOU WOULDN'T BE EMBARRASSED IF I ASKED YOU TO DO A FEW TRICKS WOULD YOU?"

Some people think that in the future dogs will overthrow their masters and will remake the world in their own image and interests. They might create olfactory theme parks smelling of compost, fish heads, and private parts—or set up policy centers committed to rethinking The Cat. To my mind, dogs have already outdone us, at least in emotional wisdom—dogs show us how unconditional love is given, along with loyalty and unselfishness.

It is true that if dogs teamed up with dolphins (who are undoubtedly smarter than everybody) they could start a New World Order. I would like to nominate my own two dogs—the shy but insistent black Labrador Ollie (a male) and the intense, energetic, and willful Border collie mix Fletcher (a female) as candidates for elected office in this new regime. I like to imagine this future with all its possibilities: dogs might choose certain humans to function as quasi-pets, for example. Let's say Newt Gingrich, Jerry Springer, Sally Jessy Raphaël, Jerry Falwell, and many writers of memoirs would sport muzzles and would have to learn simple commands ("sit," "stay," and "do NOT speak!"), although this could take some time. We're not talking about innate canine intelligence here, after all. But dogs are patient, remember. Dogs have spent time trying to domesticate humans and teach them simple tasks since the Paleolithic era. It's true, we will never catch a Frisbee between our teeth in midair at warp speed in the park or poke our quivering noses into baggage at airports in order to apprehend terrorists and save lives, but we *can* learn. Dogs would probably say that there is hope for *us*—but, alas, they have always been (and will continue to be) too kind to us.

Carol Muske

Chris Sheban

YOU ARE HEREBY INVITED TO THE FIRST ANNUAL

WORLD KENNEL CLUB

MASTERS TOURNAMENT

7–10 MARCH 2006

Entry applications must be received by 6 January

We look forward to your participation

OPEN TO ALL HUMAN RACES AND CREEDS

Natalie Beale

My Beloved Bipedal Revolutionary

The fast-paced information age sets in upon us. Humans spend more and more time communicating with each other and less time training and giving affection to their four-legged pals. Like every disaffected creature around the world, dogs, with no guidance and no responsibility, rebel. In order to create a better world for dogs everywhere, the movement grows. Dogs around the world learn to walk on two legs—thus giving them access to such forbidden treasures as the kitchen counter and the elusive doorknob. The world around us changes, as bipedal dogs leave their humans to create highly evolved dog communities. Dogs now recognize each other by sight rather than scent, rendering the age-old dog greeting an embarrassing reminder of a primitive, oppressive four-legged lifestyle.

Amy Butler

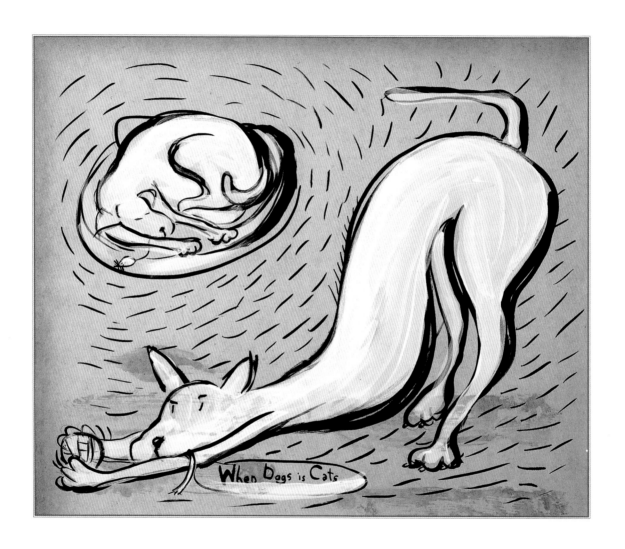

WHEN DOGS IS CATS

Genetic engineering will make it possible, I imagine, for the perfect pets to be produced. What I figure will be a hot little number is the dog-cat hybrid. Most people who like the varieties of dog shapes and sizes will go with the canine body and cat brain setup—a well-adjusted blend of catlike aloofness and litter-box independence wrapped up inside those "aw, shucks, you're the master" affectionate eyes of the domestic dog. With simple commands, your pooch will be able to go into cat mode (sleeping, eating, batting) or dog mode (chasing, scratching, howling), depending on your mood or activity. Drawbacks will be few, other than the fact that in cat mode your Great Dane hybrid may be found napping on top of your good china cupboard.

David Butler

Bill Charmatz

Michael S. Wertz

Joe's the Pick of the Litter at 2099 Dog Show

Purebred pugs, poodles, and Pomeranians were passed over yesterday when a pedigree-challenged "small brown dog" named Joe was chosen best in show at Westminster.

Although owners and breeders were reluctant to speak, judge Nicholas Foster was eager to talk about this year's surprise winner.

"We're not just a beauty contest anymore. Dogs and people have been together for a long time. This year we wanted to honor that timeless bond. We looked for the Essence of Dog, and we found it in Joe."

To which Joe's happy owner added: "Joe's a good dog. He's smart and sweet, and he comes when I call. Who could ask for anything more?"

Susan Meddaugh

Try *That* On for Size

Given the stretch of time dogs have roamed this earth, the last couple of centuries, when humans have bred dogs into fanciful shapes, seem but a mere blink . . . unless, of course, you happen to be the shar-pei puppy with more surgical stitches in his eyelids than a Palm Beach socialite, simply because excessive skin folds prevent normal blinking. Or the bug-eyed pug whose face expresses the stunning (yet constant) realization that even shallow nostril-breathing can be an intense aerobic exercise. What price glamour?

Time, as it applies to dog breeding, has been, well, *spent*. In the updated, reciprocal spirit of animal testing, twenty-first-century breeders will be required to experiment on themselves before deciding that a particular cosmetic alteration is suitable and appealing for dogs. Before too long, we can expect to see a few more wolf-like canines at the ends of diamond-studded leashes, strolling the boulevards of tony neighborhoods.

Mark Allen Svede

Kristaps Ģelzis

Across the pet care industry—from breeders
and groomers to veterinarians and trainers,
from pet-sitters and dog walkers to shelter
workers and dog wardens—the big topic
at every conference, recertification class,
and copier machine remains the same:
How will dogs look in the coming centuries?
If a few hundred years of human-controlled
breeding has created a pack of hybrids
that includes an apricot teacup poodle,
a Great Dane taller than most cars, a basset
hound that barely clears the floor, and the
pink and plume-headed Chinese crested,
what new conformations will
we come to recognize?

Mark Ulriksen

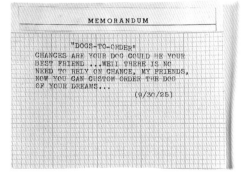

order form

I would like a dog just like me. Thank You, MAR 3 2016

IRMA WONDER

APPROVED

MEMORANDUM

"DOGS-TO-ORDER"
CHANCES ARE YOUR DOG COULD BE YOUR
BEST FRIEND ...WELL THERE IS NO
NEED TO RELY ON CHANCE, MY FRIENDS,
NOW YOU CAN CUSTOM ORDER THE DOG
OF YOUR DREAMS...

(9/30/25)

Giselle Potter

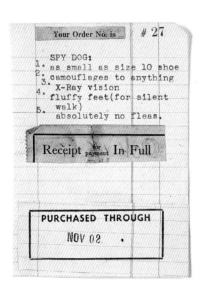

Your Order No. is __ # 27

SPY DOG:
1. as small as size 10 shoe
2. camouflages to anything
3. X-Ray vision
4. fluffy feet(for silent walk)
5. absolutely no fleas.

Receipt for payment In Full

PURCHASED THROUGH
NOV 02 .

ORDER FORM 2003

My Girls:
Twin, Toy, Tu-Tu wearing
Pink Poodles
with Water Spaniel hair

Walk on Hind legs only
Speak French fluently
Sing numerous showtunes

PAID

SPACES BELOW TO BE FILLED IN BY APPLICANT

Print Name: Earl Grins
Give Legal Residence — Street and No.
City or Post Office: Newton Falls   State N.Y.

Greg Clarke

detachable spider-gene braids (available in all sizes).

laser-etched polka'dotted Shar-Pei(time-warp optional).

a classic look recreated in crushed titanium.

Ivetta Federova

56.

a portable Dachshund wrapped in shredded resin.

Nuclear-baked Pekingese.

Cyber-shaved Afghan Borzoi styled with carbon fiber plugs.

LOW GRAVITY BREEDS

The Low Gravity Group was formed in 2850 and comprises fifteen Galactic Kennel Club–recognized space-adapted breeds. The first low-gravity breed recognized by the GKC was the ducthound, which was genetically engineered by workers in the early space stations to combat the problem of rats in station ductwork. Free from the constraints of gravity, ducthounds reach lengths of five feet (1.5 meters) and attain a maximum height of ten inches (twenty-five centimeters). Like all the Low Gravity breeds, ducthounds have extremely rough footpads, which allow them to navigate the carpeted walkways just like the Velcro-booted space pioneers. Other low-gravity breeds include the Jupiter hound, which at six feet (1.8 meters) is the tallest breed; the lunar retriever; and the station shepherd, which was the first genetically engineered breed to be recognized by the GKC.

Nirah H. Shomer

Lab Report

As the owner of a nearly one-hundred-pound yellow Lab, a popular breed, I see a demand for miniature labs on the horizon. You've seen the ads for miniature horses in magazines for the idle or merely too rich in such publications as *The Robb Report.* This may turn out to be The Big Idea of the new millennium. In fact, I'm going to stop writing this now because the patent office closes in ten minutes.

Christopher Buckley

Perhaps the power of dogs will be totally unleashed.
If so, expect to see the quintessentially canine
reinvented along with every other system—just as
chain link was superseded by invisible fences,
just as metal tags were replaced with computer
ID chips. Here, even the classic poker-playing
scene has been upgraded. Likewise, won't dogs,
no longer content with hanging their heads out
car windows, vie for the chance to feel the breezes
of higher speeds and higher altitudes? Even the
long-standing antagonism between dogs and cats
might take the form of public spectacle.
But rather than submitting to long-winded
talk show hosts or smug TV judges, might our
companions duke it out in the ring, with
pay-per-view fights every weekend?

Three Canine Upgrades

Sasha Rubel

In the twenty-first century, dogs learned that they were being replaced by cats in the hearts of pet owners everywhere. (They were only worried about survival—they had nothing against the popularity of cats. But cats, being cats, lorded it over them, strolling about with their tails up in the air like exclamation points: Look at us!)

The dogs organized the canine equivalent of phone trees to spread their message: IF WE DON'T DO SOMETHING, WE—LIKE DINOSAURS, EDSELS, AND SUSPENDERS—WILL BECOME EXTINCT.

That's when dogs stopped marrying for love and began breeding for longer and more dextrous paws. It took many more years to extend legal protection (income tax, minimum wage, etc.) to canines once their facility with cash registers and video poker machines became known.

Enid Shomer

Charlene Potts

Is Your Dog Psychic?

Does your pooch instinctively know the difference between a ride to the vet and a ride to the park?

Is he waiting at the door to greet you, even when you've been working late? Scientists have long noted the psychic connections between owners and their dogs. These connections have been dismissed for years as the projection of owners' emotions on their dogs, but recent findings confirm that dogs possess powers beyond our human comprehension. Now, after fruitless attempts at deciphering the patterns of dog hair in vacuum cleaner bags, the placement of flea bites on dog skin, and various telepathic experiments, communicators at Stanford University's Center for Canine Studies have documented and harnessed the supernatural powers of dogs.

Act now, and you and your pet can jump on the gravy train! Harness your dog's psychic powers! Help your dog realize his inherent psychic powers! Call 1-800-PSYCHIC today!

Kristin Rauchenstein

Edward Koren

Brad Holland

As space becomes more congested, urban
planners turn to Japan for solutions.
The culture that produced
bonsai sequoias and indoor golf courses
would seem to possess the solutions
for the metropolis that has nowhere
to go but up. Alas, dog racing,
a less-than-winning idea in any century
or any setting, presents problems that
even Japanese transistorization can't
solve. As one poet wrote:

high-rising windows
thin dogs leap in thinner air
off-track bets are off

In 2003, two pugs, Persil and Daphne, misplaced their owners. They settled in Central Park in Manhattan, on a hillside near Fifth Avenue at about Seventy-third Street.

The descendants of Persil and Daphne (numbering, say, thirty?) inhabit the very same hillside today. A lack of human pampering has made these pugs a little wild—some would say feral, even.

Not unlike their domestic counterparts, the Central Park pugs sleep a great deal of the time, and chase poodles some of the time, but spend most of their waking moments in ruthless pursuit of other people's lunches: a muffin, a hot dog, a bagel with cream cheese—even yogurt in a plastic container with fruit at the bottom—are all fair game for the C.P. pugs, much to the dismay of many an unsuspecting human who might have otherwise enjoyed a quiet lunch break in the park.

Victoria Roberts

Evangelia Philippidis

Dogs have accommodated unfathomable
inconsistencies in this modern world.
Some live bicoastal lives, transported in their
humans' shoulder bags aboard planes.
Some map "yards" amid grassless expanses
of traffic and pedestrians. Some even negotiate,
when their humans share custody of them,
split territories: a pied-à-terre as well as a
pied-à-ciel, connected via a temperamental
mechanical box or seven flights of stairs.

How might the future's distances and travels
corrupt a dog's instincts? Will space-traveling dogs
suffer jet lag, homesickness, seasonal affective disorder?
If dogs reside with us on the moon, will there be
howling at the full Earth? Will we all take up the
chorus, staring into the dizzying sky, wondering why
we ever launched ourselves into a solar system in
which Earth is the only planet *not* named after a god?

Friday

588 Lassie in Space (CC) - Adventure
Lassie protects Timmy from a ill-tempered Martian and also stops a thief from stealing the family's matter transporter. And all within half an hour. (R) 30 Min.

591 Air Bud XII (CC) - Comedy
After mastering nearly every sport possible, Air Bud manages to amaze yet again. But instead of basketball or sky-diving, Bud masters the art of hopscotch and takes the play grounds of the world by storm. Brendon Franklin, Kimberly Amber Smith. 85 Min. (2043)

592 Wishbone - Children In this episode Wishbone plays out the classic tale of JAWS. (R) 25 Min.

594 Homeward Bound VI (CC) - Adventure
This time around the trio of house pets get lost in their back yard and has another great adventure on their quest for the back porch. Michael J. Fox, Weezie Goldsnuff. 145 Min. (2038)

597 Doggy Duty - Serial 30 Min.

600 Do Mimes Cry? - Adventure When Americans get sick and tired of the mime menace, people start to train their dogs to take care of this problem that has gone on far too long. Cuba Gooding III, Pete Crustofski. 110 Min. (2049)

8:00 **2 Nick Knack Paddywack - Children** 30 Min.

4 Old Yeller: The Rebirth - Family Old Yeller Returns from the dead to enact foam-mouthed vengeance on his owners. Chuck Heslon, Heather Gramcracker. 120 Min. (2014)

6 Flea Boys - Serial 30 Min.

7 Dog Squad 3000 - Adventure
In a distant future where the feline species is taking over the world, mankind's only hope lies with their best friend, dog. Jake Floyd. 135 Min. (2047)

10 Bob Barker's Spay and Neuter Hour (CC) - Serial Another hour of Bob Barker's perfectly preserved head showing the proper way to spay and neuter your pets. 60 Min.

11 Dog's-Eye View (CC) - News 30 Min.

13 Bone A Petite (CC) - Instructional
Find out how to make your own apple rawhide crisp. 25 Min.

14 Fifi's Doghouse (CC) - Comedy
Join Fifi along with her friends Bowly and Captain Choke Chain for another fun-filled half hour. 30 Min.

15 Dogemite - Adventure Dogemite is released from the pound and decides to track down the flea bag that put him there. 125 Min. (2023)

16 Benji Go Away - Adventure
After wearing out his welcome, Benji is kicked out of his home. Follow the brave pooch on his adventure in the dirty slums of the big city. 90 Min. (2031)

19 Fetch This! (CC) - Comedy 30 Min.

21 Dog Days (CC) - News 30 Min.

22 12 Puppies - Drama Thanks to the army of the 12 puppies man-kind could be on the verge of extinction. The big problem is no one will stop them, because the puppies are so darn cute. Drake Ramerez, Estela Jones. 150 Min. (2042)

25 Poo Sniffer - Comedy 30 Min.

27 Kiss or Lick - Serial 25 Min.

28 Snoopy's Disco Inferno 3000 - Music
Dance the night away with Snoopy and the funky sounds of Scratch King Cole, James Bow Wow, and the Woodstock Funkmaster Dream Machine. 60 Min.

30 Dog Eat Dog World (CC) - News 60 Min.

78.

Chad Kimes

I expect to face the Brave New World with the Same Old Dog. Indeed, I fervently hope so. As I see it, there's not much room for improvement in Dog (and I have always believed: if it ain't broke, don't fix it). Indeed, Dog, as I know him, is damn near perfect.

From Dog's point of view, however (this has been gently communicated to me by my dogs, Boots and Toddles), the only drawback to the status quo is food: kibble has all the charm of industrial strength Grape Nuts. Still, even though gourmet cuisine sounds tempting—spring-green grass lightly coated with a cornmeal batter and deep-fried, tempura style; Milk Bones Bourguignonne; Dead Bird Bienville—that way lies liposuction, dieting, and self-help books.

My vision of the future is that Dog goes on—doggedly—being just the same: tail wagging, chasing a squirrel, rolling in the snow, bouncing at the gate. I want my face licked, and my lap sat in; I want the same ol' friend snuggled up with me through the next millennium. Just where I can reach out and pat him. And I think Dog wants that, too.

Candyce Barnes

Fred Gutzeit

Dogs, still unimpressed with two-dimensional imagery and the lack of olfactory developments in home entertainment, continue to block the television, insist on being let out before a commercial break, and refuse to walk themselves, even though they have long possessed the ability. A walk requires a pack, even when its taller members lag behind.

Naturally, there are some things genetic engineering, specialized breeding programs, and cutting-edge technology will not alter about the dog. For the immediate future, the smell of a wet dog, as well as the tendency of a soaked animal to spin dry beside the best-dressed person, remain unmodified, providing an odd comfort to some dog people, anyway.

Phebe Burnham

"Eye of the Hurricanine!"

In five hundred years, advances in veterinary medicine will have made it possible for your dog's life span to equal your own. There will be a need for retirement communities for dogs who outlive their human companions, and these can be very pleasant places indeed, with amusements and activities suitable for the residents (in fact, there will be humans whose occupational specialty will be the recreational needs of the geriatric dog). There will be outings, to a park or just a long drive, in buses with all the windows rolled down so everyone can stick his or her head out during the ride. Some residents who are not quite ready to retire completely may take part-time jobs visiting human hospitals and nursing homes or may apply for security positions, such as at knitting shops. There will, of course, be the few who always seem to defy aging, with not a single graying hair on the muzzle (maybe they have "a little something" done?). And there will be the genetically blessed show-offs who magically retain a shiny, full coat of fur, play tennis ball every day, and still have enough energy and desire to do embarrassing things when human visitors come. In fact, the cadres of vital, active, retired dogs could result in a powerful lobby organization that no politician would dare ignore.

Bonnie Thomas Abbott

Jonathan Schmitt

Being pack members from the get-go, dogs will seek more community-minded activities to legitimize the gang's usual hijinks at the dog park. Breeds will initially imitate the models of fraternal orders. From the Lions Club, seeing-eye dogs will assume the responsibility of collecting used eyeglasses. With a rallying pride, mixed-breed dogs will declare that no one deserves the title Odd Fellows more than they. But some things have to be retired: handshakes, especially secret ones, will prove vexing. And despite a reputation for humoring their owners' dinner guests with "stupid pet tricks," Shriner dogs will forswear driving miniature cars and sporting flowerpot hats.

Duke Norway

The old dog of the future will lie under the porch on a July afternoon and say to the human child who has crawled under there to be with him:

"These young pups today don't know what it's like to tree a possum. They don't even know enough to check the couch every morning to see if there's bits of potato chips and popcorn stuck between the cushions. I knew to do that because my dad and the older dogs taught me to. But pups today won't listen to nobody, not even when it's to their own benefit. And they're lazy. Why, they won't even eat their kibble unless it's in an anti-gravity bowl. They're too durn lazy to bend their necks.

"With those new automatic heinie-flushing devices, they don't even smell like dogs any more, so they don't sniff each other's heinies. What is a dog, just let me ask you that, what is a dog if it doesn't sniff another dog's heinie? Why, I'll tell you, he's not really a dog at all.

"But, boy, I love those flying pods. When I was a pup, you could only pee on the base of the tree! Now I shower them from above and I'm a hundred yards away before the first drop hits a leaf. And one of the biggest thrills of my life came when we took that vacation trip to the moon. I got to sit on the moon and howl at Earth! What's not to like about that?"

Andrew Hudgins

Thomas Wharton

But even beyond their duties
as members of the human pack,
could dogs begin to take a more
active role in shaping their own
destinies as well as their bodies?
Would they then be in tune with
their dreams and deepest desires?
Perhaps they could learn to
articulate desires even deeper
than the daily longing for cheese.

While in Pet therapy, Owen discovers that in Past lives he was Theda Bara, a soldier

in World War II, the inventor of a Fried Pork Rind Snack, and a 1970s Disco Dancer.

Steven Dana

Kevin Hawkes

No doubt, as with medical
advances, some technology will
eventually trickle down from
humans to dogs as well.
With no further need of
professional dog walkers,
radio collars, or even leashes,
dogs might engage their own
virtual reality walking devices,
with programmable outings such
as chasing ducks at the reservoir,
herding sheep on the moon,
and Olympic relay races.

I'm not sure what will be happening to anyone in the future, but I do know this: Whatever the technology, dogs will be swallowing pieces of it and having them removed from their intestines.

Merrill Markoe

COLLARSTAY 2.0™

Introducing CollarStay 2.0™, the latest version of our most popular software-driven beagle accessory. With CollarStay 2.0™, the beagle no longer roams wherever the wind blows—because it's all right under her nose!

CollarStay 2.0™ is an adjustable collar with remote-control programming that emits scent platforms of the owner's choosing. Thirty-two Simu-Smell™ programs—twice as many as CollarStay 1.5™!—are housed in a handsome nylon sheathing (grey heather, camel, and punch available in S, M, L; cornflower and loden in S, M only). The Scent Disseminator™ nodule releases fine spray mists in the direction of the dog's olfactory canals. New categories include chicken skin, rottweiler excreta (two versions), used Kleenex, and feet. Owners will love the palm-sized remote Kall-Back Kontrol™, which releases designated odors at the earliest sign of wanderlust, often stopping the beagle in her tracks and rendering her stationary for up to seven minutes (the average amount of time our researchers have determined necessary for locating and attaching a misplaced leash). CATALOG ONLY

Lise Funderburg

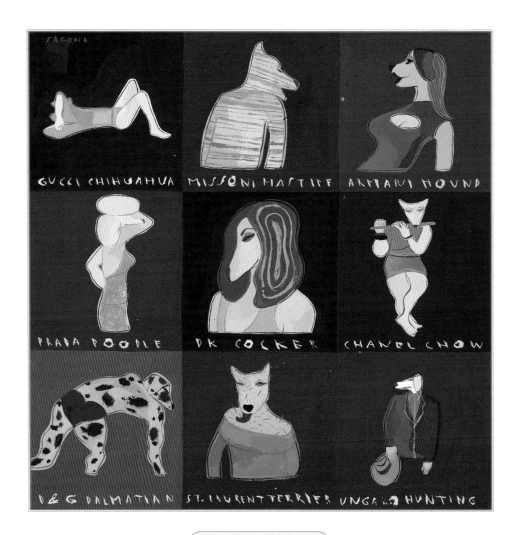

Marina Sagona

No longer satisfied with
accessorizing a full-tilt outfit
with a tony borzoi or
a pedigreed Jack Russell
(or still convinced that fur
is fabulous), designers, too,
turn their attention to an
underserved, underdressed
population of consumers:
the family dog. Hound couture
fashions appear each season
from all the best dog houses
throughout the world.

Yumi Heo

Naturally, the entire beauty and spa industry will follow suit, developing Peticure Parlors® treatment and spa facilities exclusively for discriminating dogs in need of revitalization, toning, pampering, or pure relaxation, whether that means massage, aromatherapy, seaweed wraps, customized diet and fitness regimes, or simply an hour-long belly rub. Down-market dogs will continue to pursue home treatments: do-it-yourself mud baths, daubing dead fish behind the ears, an aerobic chase of the UPS truck, etc.

NEW YORK REVIEW OF SCENT: 2/6/2032

AUTHOR QUERY

London independent research terrier is seeking confirmation that human Bangkok-Madras Olfactory Research Institute is planning seminar entitled "Apprehensions of World of Canine Poetry" after a deaf-blind honors graduate got whiff of true doggerel. Implications of human awareness are, as usual, grave, possibly dangerous, so please scent early reply.

Peter Neumeyer

Henry Horenstein

Joy Beckner

As human humility begins to outstrip human vanity, people will come to respect, and even imitate, the greater abilities and qualities that Earth's other creatures possess. Dogs, who never gloat or hold grudges, despite having all the reason in the world to do so, will generously reveal to humankind many secrets of the universe. Not so much secrets, really, as the obvious: things that our frantic lives had willfully and ceremoniously obscured.

For instance, here, two dachshunds demonstrate the passive yin and the active yang that the truly wise can recognize within everything. Previously, the uninitiated had perceived this ultimate state of harmony as merely "sleeping in."

In the vastly reduced postal system of the future, there will be far fewer mail carriers for dogs to torment. Responding to this curious canine psychosocial vacuum, a Dallas-based pet psychologist-turned-entrepreneur will market an inflatable product that looks like a cross between a mail carrier and a punching bag. This human-sized chew will bear the name Mail, Caesar!

Larger dogs, of course, will bury these neoprene items in their backyards in crude death chambers; in a 2013 TV special, *When Pets Get Their Own TV Shows*—a behind-the-scenes *Entertainment Tonight*—type program about the canine stars of reality-based TV shows—one segment will introduce us to Mr. Ruggles, a golden retriever who has fastidiously buried six Mail, Caesar! chews in sarcophagi he has fashioned out of old patio furniture.

Henry Alford

Dede Hatch

Robert Zimmerman

There's no downplaying
the fact that some twenty-
first-century dogs are clearly
not amused by change, not
tolerant of it, and simply
not stable because of it.
Just as humans revised the
four food groups into the
food pyramid in the late
twentieth century, dogs,
too, will decide that a
varied diet is best.

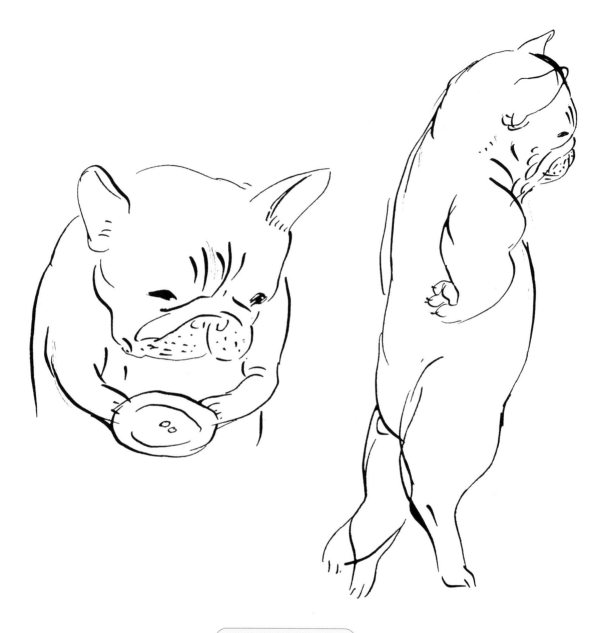

Vivienne Flesher

Dogs will now be fed only free-range, organic, pure, antibiotic-free, pesticide-free, natural, fresh living flesh.

No beans.

Nothing from tins.

If these requirements go unmet, dogs will stalk from your house in a huff, which will be easy, since they will now have their own keys.

Cynthia Heimel

Christian Clayton

Many dogs, shucking the stereotypes of what a dog's life is or isn't, pursue aesthetic goals, including careers in opera, ballet, and the visual arts. And, truth to tell, when it comes to technique, the difference between a pirouette and chasing one's tail is rather negligible. At academic conferences, dogs are now shown to have had their own "Hollywood" era, complete with glamorous stars, fan clubs, and classic movie roles.

Further reforms will be initiated, hoping to more accurately represent the aesthetic contributions of dogs.

Robin Schwartz

Julianne Taaffe

Dogs of the Future from a Recent Past Perspective

Movie Memo, 1967, Jay Ventura to Gregor Greenberg

Greeny: Just watched the rough cut of the untitled Charlton Heston project. First of all, let me tell you—I love it. Love, love, *love* it.

Having said that, allow me to humbly heft some studio notes your utterly brilliant way. First: Does it have to be *another planet?* And does it have to be *dogs?* We're crazy about the scenes where Chuck has his shirt off. That's gonna play like Pop Tarts in Peoria. But those Pooch People beating our hero with rolled-up newspapers? That's gotta be disturbing to your average pet owner— and, let's face it, Greeny, that's pretty much *every goddamn moviegoer in North America!*

The nose and ear prosthetics on the Super Mutts look great—though I bet it didn't take much to make Mickey Rooney look like a pug! *Ha ha!* (By the way, lose him. He stinks up the place like a wet weimaraner.) But *Greeny, Greeny, Greeny*—real human people are comfortable with *themselves* being the masters and the *dogs* being the nonmasters (or the slaves, or the production assistants, or whatever you'd call it). For most of these flyover schmucks, dogs are the only thing they *are* masters of. And, yes, I know, *I know.* You're doing a thought-provoking switcheroo thing here. We just need a little less of the thought and a lot less of the provoking.

I promise you, you Einstein-and-Eisenstein-rolled-into-one, that Twentieth Century Fox is still *deeply committed* to the concept of Animals Running

Steven O'Donnell

Civilization While Top Talent Clad in Mini-Rags Fall in Love in a Cage. But how about, say, *turtles?* Edward Everett Horton would look perfect in a shell. Or maybe *fish?* I'll have my people look into the availability of Don Knotts and Edward G. Robinson.

As they took the muzzle off Heston, I got goose bumps when he shouted, *"Take your hands off me, you damn dirty dachshund!"* So perfect! Especially since Roddy McDowell looks like a sad-eyed wiener dog even out of makeup! All I ask is that you change the situation completely.

Some last thoughts: I want to repeat that working with you and Charlton is, for me, like working with God *and* Moses! But remember, even God screwed up with flops like the mosquito, Jerry Van Dyke, and *Cleopatra.*

As everybody knows, and as I have actually heard people say at testimonial dinners in honor of me, I like to be *positive.* It was absolutely edge-of-seat time when Heston screams oh-so-scarily, "Soylent Kibble is *people!"* But you know what? It's another whole story. Pull it out of this picture *pronto.*

So, Greeny—get this picture on track. Or else, Big Idea Boy, it won't be just the frisky Space Collies that get "fixed."

And, hey! You could even consider *cats.* Sure, they're common pets—but bottom line? Nobody really trusts 'em.

In the realm of history, particularly art history, the role of the dog is being reevaluated—some might say overturned. Some strident members of the academic community advocate the abolition of speciesist words such as "it" and advocate a new gender/species neutral term, "s/h/it," to be used instead of the "s/he" that failed to gain universal adoption. This early work by Gerrit van Honthorst, *Supper with a Lute Player,* demonstates that companion animals were often used by many of the Old Masters, who found human models less comfortable with the "stay" command.

Melinda Copper

LAST KNOWN VAN GOGH PAINTING FOUND

21 June 2118 (London): It has been more than twenty-five years since scholars discovered a painting by Vincent Van Gogh that had been presumed lost. This particular painting, the subject of which is a dog, was located by a French farmer in a doghouse that dates back to Van Gogh's own time period (approximately 1885). Remarkably preserved by mud, the painting had apparently hung in the doghouse itself.

Van Gogh speaks of this work and its origins in a remarkable letter to his brother, Theo, dated some two hundred years ago. (A facsimile of the original letter is reprinted at right.)

This work, being the only authentic Van Gogh painting scholars had been unable to find, is considered priceless.

Lori McElrath-Eslick

Michael Plank

WALKING

I was out walking with a couple of friends the other day—including a real cute heeler who thinks she's so smart! Well . . . she is—and the people who were with us started talking about the millennium (two of them even got the year right) and how the world was going to change, and all the plans they had, and all, and it occurred to us that if they'd just relax and take nice long walks and nuzzle and smell each other everything would go along just fine and everything would be both simpler and a lot friendlier, and that the whole concept of millennium and numbers in general and holidays and all the rest is—how did the cute bitch put it?—"arbitrary."

Then we got to talking about the fact that most restaurants (except in France, maybe) are politically incorrect in that they won't let us in to see that the people don't eat too much, and what do these millennium people plan to do about that in this millennium of theirs?

All in all, a good walk.

Edward Albee

Dogs were dogs before they were domestic dogs. And in the absence of leashes, collars, cement, chain link, Vari Kennels, and the like, they did what no other species has done (though some of them—the cat, for example—observed the process and got on the bandwagon): dogs domesticated us. Or, if you prefer, the process was reciprocal, but it would certainly have been impossible without a great deal of active and thoughtful interest in the process of civilization as they moved forward, with their large hearts, making ever more room for our cave drawings, our houses (now rodent free!), our department stores, and schoolhouses.

Civilization began with dogs and, perhaps one day, it will end with dogs.

Vicki Hearne

Eric Hanson

When all has been said and done,
when the future has run its course
and we humans have done our
darnedest to keep up (and not
let on that we're out of breath),
dogs will still be by our sides,
on our beds, and under our feet,
gazing up at our faces as though
we were all the future, all the
cosmos, all the progress and space
and time they'd ever known or ever
dreamed of knowing. Perhaps, one
day in the coming centuries, we'll
even deserve such companions.
Both parties can hope.

Robin Bowman

Richard Cowdrey

CREDITS

Pages 1, 4, 6-7, 8, 11, 12, 14: art copyright ©2000 Anne Watkins; pages 22, 30, 58, 59, 94-95, 115: art copyright © 2000 Matthew Yokom; pages 15, 29, 50, 60, 73, 77, 82, 86, 90, 93, 97, 99, 103, 107, 111, 116, 124: text copyright © 2000 Michael J. Rosen and Mark Allen Svede; page 3: art copyright © 2000 Jeffrey Fisher; page 5: art copyright © 2000 Stephen Webster; page 16: text copyright © 2000 Erin McGraw; page 17: art copyright © 2000 Benoit; pages 18-19: art copyright © 2000 Danny Shanahan; pages 20-21: text and art copyright © 2000 Matthew Yokom; page 22-23: text copyright © 2000 Andy Borowitz; pages 24-25: text and art copyright © 2000 Janet Stevens; pages 26-27: text and art copyright © 2000 Paul Lindhorst; page 28: art copyright © 2000 Mary Lynn Blasutta; pages 30-31: text copyright © 2000 Arthur Yorinks; pages 32-35: art copyright © 2000 Charles Barsotti; page 36: text copyright © 2000 Carol Muske; page 37: art copyright © 2000 Chris Sheban; pages 38-39: art copyright © 2000 Natalie Beale; pages 40-41: text and art copyright © 2000 Amy Butler; pages 42-43: text and art copyright © 2000 David Butler; page 44: art copyright © 2000 Bill Charmatz; page 45: art copyright © 1999 Michael S. Wertz; pages 46-47: text and art copyright © 2000 Susan Meddaugh; page 48: text copyright © 2000 Mark Allen Svede; page 49: art copyright © 2000 Kristaps Ģelzis; page 51: art copyright © 1999 Mark Ulriksen; pages 52-54: art copyright © 2000 Giselle Potter; page 55: art copyright © 2000 Greg Clarke; pages 56-57: art copyright © 2000 Ivetta Federova; page 58: text copyright © 2000 Nirah H. Shomer; page 59: text copyright © 2000 Christopher Buckley; pages 61-63: art copyright © 2000 Sasha Rubel; page 64: text copyright © 2000 Enid Shomer; page 65: art copyright © 2000 Charlene Potts; pages 66-67: text and art copyright © 2000 Kristin Rauchenstein; pages 68-71: art copyright © 2000 Edward Koren; page 72: art copyright © 1980 Brad Holland; pages 74-75: text and art copyright © 2000 Victoria Roberts; page 76: art copyright © 2000 Evangelia Philippidis; pages 78-79: text and art copyright © 2000 Chad Kimes; page 80: text copyright © 2000 Candyce Barnes; page 81: art copyright © 2000 Fred Gutzeit; page 83: art copyright © 2000 Phebe Burnham; page 84: text copyright © 2000 Bonnie Thomas Abbott; page 85: art copyright © 2000 Jonathan Schmitt; page 87: art copyright © 2000 Duke Norway; page 88: text copyright © 2000 Andrew Hudgins; page 89: art copyright © 2000 Thomas Wharton; page 91: text and art copyright © 2000 Steven Dana; page 92: art copyright © 2000 Kevin Hawkes; page 94: text copyright © 2000 Merrill Markoe; page 95: text copyright © 2000 Lise Funderburg; pages 96-97: art copyright © 2000 Marina Sagona; page 98: art copyright © 2000 Yumi Heo; page 100: text copyright © 2000 Peter Neumeyer; page 101: art copyright © 1998 Henry Horenstein; page 102: art copyright © 2000 Joy Beckner, photograph by Marty Keeven; page 104: text copyright © 2000 Henry Alford; page 105: art copyright © 2000 Dede Hatch; page 106: art copyright © 2000 Robert Zimmerman; page 108: art copyright © 2000 Vivienne Flesher; page 109: text copyright © 2000 Cynthia Heimel; page 110: art copyright © 2000 Christian Clayton; page 112: art copyright © 2000 Robin Schwartz; page 113: art copyright © 2000 Julianne Taaffe; pages 114-115: text copyright © 2000 Steven O'Donnell; page 117: art copyright © 2000 Melinda Copper; pages 118-119: text and art copyright © 2000 Lori McElrath-Eslick; page 120: art copyright © 2000 Michael Plank; page 121: text copyright © 2000 Edward Albee; page 122: text copyright © 2000 Vicki Hearne; page 123: art copyright © 2000 Eric Hanson; page 125: art copyright © 2000 Robin Bowman; page 126: art copyright © 2000 Richard Cowdrey.

ACKNOWLEDGMENTS

Genuine thanks are extended to all the artists and writers who donated their efforts for this book in order to provide emergency or ongoing care for companion animals, and to each agency The Company of Animals Fund has assisted with these grants over the last decade.

Specific appreciation goes to four individuals and institutions who encouraged and facilitated the creation of this volume: Barbara Jedda and the AKC Museum of the Dog, Walter King and the Columbus College of Art & Design, Teresa Shelley and Riley Illustration, and Cameron Woo and *Bark* Magazine.

"The Future Dog!"

—an exhibition of contemporary drawings represented in this publication—

was commissioned by the American Kennel Club Museum of the Dog

with the kind support of the American Kennel Club.

A selection of forty-five works of art is reserved for display

in St. Louis, Missouri, beginning on October 1, 2000,

and is available at subsequent venues for exhibit.